The Wild Inside

A Memoir

Sodasia Thompson

QUILL HAWK PUBLISHING

Cover Design by Ava Wood, Fins and Feathers Designs

Cover Art by Sodasia Thompson

ISBN: 978-1-965142-14-1 (Hardback)

ISBN: 978-1-965142-13-4 (Paperback)

Library of Congress Control Number: 2024918493

QUILL HAWK PUBLISHING

Disclaimer

This memoir reflects my personal experiences and emotions based on real events. While the narrative is rooted in true occurrences, it may include elements of creative interpretation to enhance the storytelling. The intent is to convey the essence of my journey and the feelings associated with it. Any resemblance to actual persons or events is not coincidental, but the portrayal may be adjusted to serve the narrative's purpose and impact.

This is my story.

DISCLAIMER

CONTENTS

"I went to the woods because I wished to live deliberately, and see if I could not learn what it had to teach."

—Henry David Thoreau

PROLOGUE

The canvas boasts of magic, spectacles never before seen, and it is perfectly in its right. Still cloaked in dark blues and charcoal black streaks, the sky sheepishly yields the promise of a new day as the first timid rays of sunlight delicately brush the horizon.

I take a small, quiet breath. "Here it comes."

As if ignited by the spark of a flint, the sun bursts forth like a bolt of lightning, commanding the sky with its radiance.

It races across the heavens with incomparable speed, a symphony of orange and pink sailing out from behind. It hijacks my senses, yet I remain liberated, taken up only in a breathless spell of awe and gratitude. I lean my wet body against the overturned boat invitingly. And as the sun's warmth wraps me fully, a strange yet beautiful sensation lights up in my chest—I believe it is hope.

Here, in this remote and untamed wilderness, I am humbled by the sheer magnificence of nature's truths and possibilities. What a grand reminder of the incredible beauty and resilience that surrounds us, and a testament to the unwavering spirit of life itself. A testament to our own unwavering spirits, and who we are always capable of choosing to be. If only, day after day, year after year, moment to moment, we dare to rise like the sun.

"Adapt or perish, now as ever."

—H.G. Wells

1. Rescued

"You need to come get this baby ***now***."

The stranger's call would save my life. Not only that, but it would seal my fate, for better or worse. They didn't know me. I would never know them. And as for the better or worse part, that was yet to be decided. Because I wouldn't figure out for several years just how rescued I was.

My mother was one to numb out any semblance of a feeling. Feelings were bad, and life was worse. As drugs got harder, life grew riskier. Babies popped into the world one after the other, and who was less fit to care for them than she was.

To be honest, I never really knew my mother or my father. Though based on her track record, I could imagine the type of person she had turned out to be. All I know is that I happened. And I'd have to deal with the echo of who they were and who they weren't for the rest of my life.

The story goes that an innocent little baby, some eight months old, once lay in a tiny stroller in the middle of a cold, foreign woods in New York. Her mother, arched over her infant body, stood with an unknown man who was not the child's father. Such a context was, of course, suspicious, suggestive, and dangerous. It was at that moment that a rightfully concerned onlooker made the urgent call. Hastily, the baby was rescued by her Aunt Cee and whisked away to the quaint little home Aunt Cee owned in suburban New York. There, she would raise the baby girl until the girl was big enough to raise herself. Aunt Cee would call herself Mother. The girl would do the same.

I bet you've realized that the baby is me.

And I bet you're waiting for the happily ever after.

It's complicated.

This sort of thing would happen a grand total of four times over the span of many years, new siblings each finding their way into the shrinking home. What we needed to survive was given: food, water, and a place to lay our heads. Beyond that, however, is where the twists start to turn.

I don't know why she did it, and I never really thought to ask her. It turns out I didn't really need to because, in my lifetime, I would never be allowed to forget it. Though her heart was in the right place, Aunt Cee's mind was far, far from it. I believe she loved us. Deep in her core, she must have felt some sort of purpose, right? I mean, after all, what a noble, selfless thing she had done...

The price was high. My debt was great.

When things were good, they were good. Success in school and all was well. Good grades, awards, doing something with your life? You were loved. But everything always had to be perfect.

If it wasn't... if I wasn't... cue the hurricane. I'm big, you're small. I'm right, you're wrong. And there's nothing you or anybody else can do about it. In fact, turn your voice *off*.

Amidst the daily chaos, every moment felt uncertain. Unstable. I never knew what would come my way, and tension hung thick in the air, like the calm before a storm. Pretty soon, a single footstep of hers triggered urgent commands in my brain: Run. Cover. Duck. Hide. Fly. Freeze. But never fight.

Aunt Cee expected unwavering compliance, a surrender of self—a standard impossible to meet. A misplaced dish or a slightly askew bedsheet could ignite the hurricane, not of wind and rain, but of anger and fury.

A constant tick-tick-tick-tick filled the halls. I became a small figure, a skilled tightrope walker in a minefield, the only way to survive the tempest. The calm at the center was an illusion, and tranquility was never truly found.

In the safety of my smallness, my voice dissolved. Speaking up wasn't an option; dissent was swiftly extinguished like a survivor's torch. There was no chance for the prize of freedom, of being heard, felt, or loved without the conditions of my surrender. The home that was meant to be a haven turned into an island. I felt deserted, and as my resentment grew, I had no one to turn to but myself.

"We are all searching for something,
even if we don't know what it is.
What we seek is what we are."

—Anonymous

2. HORIZON PINES

It is the year 2016, I am in my sophomore year of college, and I am lost. I'm in a major that I don't feel passionate about, my family is completely dysfunctional, and I have no money. The only jobs available for kids like me are either waiting tables, working summer camps, or delivering pizzas. I hate all of those things. Especially working with kids. Since I was a little girl, I've always said, "I'll never work with kids ever. I'll never have any either. I vow it." I never wanted to end up like my mother. Hating herself. Hating every day of her life. Hating me.

So why am I, on this hot summer day, taking a bus from Brooklyn to the New Jersey wilderness to spend the summer as a camp counselor? I have no idea, but it will change my life forever.

The bus rumbles along the winding black roads, pulling us further and further away from the concrete jungle I call home. The cityscape fades into a blur of green, and I am officially alone in an unknown place. My stomach churns with a mix of anxiety and anticipation as the strangers in the other rows exchange giddy get-to-know-you's. I am not there yet. The camp is a world away from the chaos I am used to, nestled in canopies and creatures and calmness.

My life is anything but calm.

In no time at all we arrive and ease our yellow school bus onto the one-hundred-acre Jersey plot. The trees seem to close their branches behind us like doors while everything before them disappears.

The humid summer air wastes no time as the scent of pine and earth fills my lungs. We file off the bus and the place is instantly alive with activity; other counselors unloading their bags, the distant sound of laughter echoing over the hilly terrain. It is overwhelming. But I follow suit, quickly snatching up my own things and trying to stay out of everyone's way. I am alone here. There is nothing and no one to tether myself to in this place. What am I doing here?

A tall, blonde woman wearing black framed glasses greets us. "Welcome to Horizon Pines! My name's Holly, and I'll be your camp director." She proceeds to promise us an "unforgettable summer" filled with "adventure" and "personal growth." They sound more like empty promises to me; or maybe that's how I want to hear them. I still don't know what has called me to this place. So I nod along, trying to mask my skepticism.

Other staff stand around in green t-shirts holding colored signs with our names on them. We split into groups across the great lawn for something called "experiential." Basically, the first part of our training as newbies will be to start as "campers" ourselves. We are to spend three days going through the typical motions of a camper to get a real feel for what this summer will be like for them. I now belong to the group called Big Dipper.

This does not sound exciting.

Each group has "counselors." Lilah and Dev are mine. Lilah is a pretty black woman in her mid-twenties, while Dev is tall, dark, and lean. They seem nice. I am happy to be around people that look like me.

They take us down a steep path, up over a small hill, and deep into the woods to find our small camp. A short, rocky trail leads us to a clearing where rustic longhouse-style dwellings are arranged. They look like they've been there forever.

"This is it!" Dev says excitedly, stretching his arms out wide in the center of the clearing.

I take a peek inside the shelters, and the mood shift is palpable. I am silent. The bed is hard and covered in a thin layer of dust. Bugs crawl around the edges, and the structure, a hogan, is open on both sides, exposing me to the elements. The green plastic mattress covering is ripped in four places, exposing a spongy yellow foam. The blankets and sheets are "Horizon Pines" clean, and the mosquito net has ten holes in it patched with duct tape. The forest is all around me, and the sounds of nature are loud. I try to breathe, to not freak out, but it's getting harder and harder because there's nothing I can do. I am here now. I committed to this. And this is not something I think I can do.

I try some grounding exercises and finally start to notice the people around me. We exchange polite nods and smiles, but everyone seems as unsettled as I am, exchanging wary glances, taking in their surroundings, and trying to adjust to this new reality. A chorus of cicadas fills the silence between us. Dev finally clears his throat and invites us to circle up around the fire pit.

"I know it doesn't look like much, and some of you might be freaking out." Yes, Dev, analyze me. I'm freaking out. "But there's something special about this place. It's hard to explain, but it changes you. Time moves differently here. When you're detached from your phone and the world outside, your body makes a shift too. Many friends that have passed through these woods say it was here that, for the first time, they met themselves."

His words linger in my mind. As lost as I am, I've always made it my mission to know myself more deeply, to find my way out. But perhaps there's something more. Maybe there's a puzzle piece, a crooked, missing shape buried deep in these woods, that I'm meant to find. Perhaps it's waiting for me.

We finish arranging the last of our belongings and make the long trek back up the hill to the great hall. This is where all of our meals will be served. It's an enormous, handmade log cabin filled with large wooden tables and benches. It smells one hundred years old, but that's good to me. We take our seats, trying to catch our breath. Holly raises a hand, which we quickly learn means mouths off, eyes up. She begins:

"Welcome, everyone, to Horizon Pines! As you will come to know, this camp is unlike any other in the world. And our kids are some of the best around.

We work hard to create a camp program that's inclusive and financially accessible to all. Our population of campers comes mainly from all over New York City. They are a beautiful blend of races, ethnicities, gender identities, and economic statuses. Fifty-one percent of the families we serve fall below the self-sufficiency standard. Many of them come from neighborhoods where they've rarely seen trees or had the chance to unplug from the harsh realities of their lives. Several of our friends have experienced trauma, live in low-income housing, or face challenges most people can't even imagine."

She pauses, her eyes scanning our faces, trying to gauge our understanding. I shift uncomfortably, the weight of her words pressing down on me. It feels like she's describing my own childhood. It hurts my chest in some places.

"But this camp isn't just about giving kids a break from their daily struggles," she continues. "It's about changing lives. We want to give kids the chance to discover who they are, to understand their world, and build their own values for life. We want them to become deep thinkers, reflectors, leaders, and doers. At the forefront of everything we do is our commitment to helping kids develop the skills and moral compasses they need to thrive as adults. And summer after summer, what we have learned to be true is this: Horizon Pines works. I want you to understand how important you are in making this happen. How essential your presence is. I want you to know that this is as much for you as it is for them. I am your director, yes, but you will be their everything. And I am so glad you are here."

The room is silent. Her words take their time in the air, and we let them. Postures soften while heads bob up and down in understanding. A warm rush of empathy begins to pour over my anxiety. I think more than anything in this world, we are all on a quest to figure out where we belong.

"These kids deserve a summer that will stick with them for life," Holly breaks, her voice softening. "Just like the people around this room, you never know what someone may carry in the load on their back. But it's our job to help lighten that load, even if just for a summer."

I can't help but drift away. The rhythmic gusts of the ceiling fans send me back in my mind to my own burdens, the weight of my family's dysfunction, the feeling of being lost, the hopelessness. Perhaps in helping someone else, I can find some way out of my own darkness.

Clanging pots in the kitchen pull me back to the humid space. Holly smiles. It is a deep, genuine smile. "You're here for a reason, even if you don't know what it is yet. This place has a way of revealing things to you. Trust the process, and trust yourselves."

I take a deep breath. Trust myself. How could I manage a thing like that when everything bad that's ever happened to me is all my fault?

The rest of the evening is a blur of introductions and small talk. I learn the layout of the camp, take my first wilderness shower and try to absorb as much information as possible. My mind keeps drifting back to Holly's words.

I make pictures in my mind of those kids. I see their faces. I see mine too.

As I lay my body down on that hard, dusty bed that night, I remember I have no idea what I'm doing here. But then I think about what little me would have wanted, what little me had always needed.

I figure that's a good place to start.

"Coming together is a beginning,
staying together is progress,
and working together is success."

—Henry Ford

3. A Song for Breakfast

It's an interesting second day at Horizon Pines. Us "campers" are woken up bright and early, at 5:30 in the morning to be exact! It is a hard rule to be at breakfast before the morning bell rings at 6. Sleep wasn't terrible the night before, but maybe I was just too exhausted to fixate on what crawly creatures could jump into my hogan and make their way into my sleeping bag. We are up and dressed in all of five minutes, then Lilah and Dev briefly check in with us about the day. We set some personal goals, check for ticks and head out.

I've never sat with my family for a meal. Not a real one anyway, like the ones they show in the movies: Dad asks Mom to pass the peas, Little Brother sneaks a pinch at Sister's arm, and she rolls her eyes in return. But they sit, and they eat, and they say, "I love you."

I mean, of course, we have Thanksgiving in my house, like any other family. Except it's not like any other family. We hold hands, we pray, then we take our overloaded plates to our different corners of the house and eat by ourselves.

I've always wanted my family to feel like a "real" one. What I really mean, perhaps, is a functional one. Growing up, I always thought sharing meals around a table would be the magic formula to make it happen. At Horizon Pines, not only is every meal served this way, but there's table etiquette, too. And it's very important.

Some campers help set the table while others serve the food. Everyone's allowed to eat only after a table grace song has been sung. It's not religious. No one can have seconds until everyone's eaten their firsts. That's just polite. And if someone starts a song, everyone stops to listen. You can sing along too if you want. Turns out there is so much beautiful music sung here all the time. This is my favorite part of camp so far.

Music has been and always will be everything to me. It is my lifeline. At school, I am able to make something of myself by singing and performing. I've been in bands, choirs, and orchestras my entire life, and it is in those spaces where I've always been able to find real connections. It is in those spaces with those mentors and those friends where I feel like *me*.

Breakfast is served, and between the eggs, toast, and cereal bowls being passed across the wooden table, I find myself more at ease than yesterday. I'm sitting next to my group member, Kya, who tells me the milk is just right. I believe her. Kya sleeps next to me in my hogan. We may have trauma-bonded over our first night in the wilderness together. Kya is odd in a good way. She's got enough energy for ten people wound up in a skinny white frame, and she wears thick, blue glasses. I want to ask her what "just right" milk means, but before I can, Lilah lowers her fork to her plate and sings:

"Tumba, ka-tumba, tumba, ka-tumba, tumba, ka-tumba, tumba, ka-tumba..."

Instantly, an ethereal chant sweeps out across the dining hall as we lower our silverware to the tables. I don't know the song yet, so I just listen. And what a beautiful, thrumming pulse it is. It must be some African language, I think. They build louder and louder, adding a soothing melody over top. I am entranced and warm, and no longer hungry.

Suddenly, in the heartbeat of their rhythm, I am plucked away from the dining hall in the woods and thrust back to my childhood home—a home in which the family ties I was born into felt more like ropes of conditional love... twisted and tightly bound into suffocating knots. In my mind, I feel their stifling grip, cutting off the breath of my being like a serpent coiling around its prey.

Freedom died in that place.

As long as I was compliant, useful, and well-behaved, I was loved. As long as I stayed out of trouble, didn't break anything, kept the windows closed in winter, and avoided any mistakes, I was loved. *Don't let bullies touch you*, Aunt Cee would say. *Don't complain about being beaten. Don't cry when it happens either. What happens in this house stays in this house.* In other words, don't get in the way. Don't show ungratefulness. Don't ask for trust. Don't lie. *You are a liar, remember?* Don't ask for anything—not rides or money—don't need anything and don't want too much either.

It's not worth it.

But outside my home, in the real world, in the safer world, in the presence of strangers, I was free. In my mentors and peers, education and music, I learned trust. I practiced it and cultivated the skill of leaning in with others to break out of myself. When teachers gave me feedback, I ran toward them, not away. I'd droll on to the parents I babysat for, painting vivid pictures of normal happenings in my life that most certainly were not. They'd listen and thank me and guide me. I didn't know it, but they were parenting me too. Because of strangers, I discovered that leaning into discomfort makes way for hope. And that learning of the self and the world is the foundation of a good life.

The forest out here at first glance may appear empty, but in shared joy like this, I find fullness. As they end, their voices reach the deepest places of my mind and tug me back into the center of the dining hall. And I am grateful. I believe the opposite of scarcity is not abundance; it is connection. And I think connection propels us forward with the assurance that, no matter the challenge, someone else is there. It helps us be better people, better family members, and better friends.

We snap our fingers like a round of applause to celebrate the music, then the chatter picks up again. Kya leans over and nudges me with her elbow, her blue glasses slipping slightly down her nose.

"So, what do you think? Milk's perfect, right?" she asks.

I stifle a laugh, shaking my head at the ridiculousness of it all. "You know, I never really thought about it before, but yeah, it's pretty spot on."

Kya beams, taking another triumphant sip. "Told you! Got no clue what they put in this stuff but Horizon Pines' milk is the best."

"If that's the case, maybe this summer won't be so bad after all."

She cackles, and I can't hold mine back any longer. I guess one of the good parts about being lost is you belong no place, and you belong every place, too.

I take another bite of my cereal.

The milk really does taste good.

"True belonging and self-worth
are not goods.
We don't negotiate their value
with the world."

—Brene Brown

4. HEAVYWEIGHT CHAMPION

"Alright everyone," Dev starts as we funnel out of the great hall after breakfast. There's a clear purpose in his tone. "Today is all about relationships and trust—both with each other and with yourselves. Getting your campers to see themselves as humans who are capable of hard things is going to be your biggest job this summer. We can't do that without seeing that in ourselves first. So the day is gonna work like this: We're going to tackle some team-building exercises, first starting with some low-touch activities, then we'll move on to the high ropes course. Yes, high ropes on day two—we're not messing around."

Little do we know, we're about to meet the Lizard King.

Our group floods out into a large field where the first set of activities awaits us. The sun's orange rays peek through the bushy tree canopies, and I take a picture in my mind to save it for later. It's beautiful here in this place. I want to bottle it up and keep it in my back pocket for a bad day.

Lilah tells us the first phase's exercises are designed to encourage communication, ice breaking and relationships. Birthdays and occupations and hobbies begin to fly around as we play silent line up games, two truths and a lie, and "twenty-question tag." We play "shrinking island" where the entire group has to continuously try to remain on top of a picnic blanket that keeps getting folded in half. Finally, we try holding pencils between our fingertips to make a circle and do all kinds of movements, keeping the pencils in place. Kya almost loses her milk on that one; she can't stop laughing. By the end of it all we are covered in smiles and dirt. It turns out the Big Dipper group's got some pretty interesting characters.

Malik is a black chemistry teacher from Brooklyn. We're just about the same age, give or take a few months. He is a softer-spoken guy, but huge in a jovial kind of way, like the planet Jupiter. I can tell he will be a strength for our group. Arun is a tall, lean, and charismatic Indian man. His smile is as wide as the sun, and he is full of palpable energy. It makes sense when he tells us he's a performer. I get the feeling we'll get along.

Amelia is a teaching assistant from Manhattan. She has long brown hair, fair skin, and a beautiful face. Her eyes say she is full of many tricks; I'd like to know what they are. And Javier is the oldest of us all. He's a twenty-eight-year-old Latin American aerospace technician with a huge family. You can tell he's got kids, too, because he gives total and complete dad vibes. Not in a bad way though. It's endearing, like he's wired to protect. He is funny. We like the same type of music.

"Grab some water everybody and take a breather. We're about to move onto phase two." Dev peels off with Lilah to grab some harnesses and helmets from a dilapidated shed nearby. We seem to sit a little closer together while waiting for them.

They return with our gear and we help one another get dressed. "Follow us," they say in strange unison, and lead us down a crooked nearby path into another clearing.

Javier gasps for all of us. "Oh... My... God."

"Everyone, meet the Lizard King."

An enormous course, twisting and intimidating like a serpent, stretches high above us. I can't even see the top as it seems to reach the clouds. The structure is daunting, with sandbags, ropes, and platforms all criss-crossing thirty feet off the ground. Its presence sends disbelief through team Big Dipper. I want to throw up. I want to hide. But there really isn't any turning back now.

Alarm bells ring out in my head like a school fire drill. How am I ever going to make it up there? I have always been the heaviest in my class, my grade, my school. I can't even do a single push-up. But there's not enough time in a moment like this to consider not giving it my best, no matter how impossible it seems. And believe me, it seems impossible.

I turn to Dev, my voice shaking, "We have to do this one by one?"

"You'll find out when the challenge begins."

Shoot. I can't even conceptualize my very certain doom.

"As you can see," Dev continues, "this course is designed to test your teamwork. We are going to push you. This may even break you. You'll be chained together and must move through it as one unit. For the first part of the course, you'll all need to ascend a steep platform. Then each of you will be responsible for moving one of these chained sandbags through the poles over the bridge to the other side. You'll descend from the bridge and finally pull one final heavy red eft over the last wall. All teammates must get over the wall with the newt to complete the course. How you start, how you progress, and how you finish is completely up to you. You've spent the morning getting to know each other. But can you show up for each other?"

The silence is so thick I can hear my dry swallow.

"I'll give you a second to discuss how you want to approach this. You have two minutes, then you will clip in and begin."

Those two minutes are the shortest of my life. I know I'll need extra support to get up and over and through everything. What if they don't want me in their group after this? What if I burden them? What if I lose my footing and hurt someone else? It's too late to worry. Time's up, and we are ushered to the starting line. Pause. Quiet. Breathe. Lilah takes her mark.

"Trust your team. Trust yourself. Trust us."

"Ready? GO!"

I see the pistol smoke in my mind's eye, and like a racehorse, we take off. Blinders are on. We run with every ounce of anything that we have. Malik is in front, followed by Kya, then Arun, Amelia, myself, and Javier as the caboose. Each of us instinctively grips the slack between us, looking back to see that the person behind us is close and secure. The platform is steep, but in counting our steps and running in unison we sail to the top with ease.

"One, two, three!" I shout as we start the next phase: sandbags. Big Dipper comes alive. We are in perfect synchronicity; no move made by a single person but as a nuclear hub. It is not easy. The sandbags are dirty and heavy and smell like forest sweat. Amelia's starts to drift from her shoulder but I block it with mine just in time. "Jesus, girl, thanks."

We drop our bags, take a deep breath, and assess the next phase. It is a shaky bridge with missing beams and ropes hanging in every possible cross-section to block us from getting across smoothly.

"That's it Big Dipper, you are whipping through this! Don't stop now!" Lilah's voice ripples over the wind through the course. I am invigorated.

Before we start, Kya takes a pause. "Hold up," she says as she zeroes in on the ropes, noticing a pattern. "Guys, see how the ropes sort of form a star shape? If we stay way low and take our steps together, we can cruise right through the middle."

The team nods. "Right on, Kya. You count us in, then we'll follow your lead."

"One. Two. Left. Right." Kya is confident and focused, and in seconds, we are through.

Dev cups his sweaty hands around his mouth and shouts to us from the other side of the wall. "This is the last part of your challenge today. Make it happen and victory is yours."

Our team descends the bridge and finally meets the base of the enormous wall. I am feeling my power grow in this place with these people. Before us in all his glory sits the Lizard King himself—a large red eft with bloodshot eyes. Every single part of this course feels impossible, but I cannot allow myself to go over the self-doubt list Aunt Cee curated personally for me: Fat, pig, animal.

The team dips low to claim the beast. He must be 200 pounds. My knees buckle under the weight but the tail begins to crush Javier, so I push harder under the belly of the lizard. Sweat burns my eyes and forces them shut. My lungs are on fire. But I do not wane.

Then suddenly out of nowhere I hear it. Amelia starts to sing. It's that song from breakfast.

How she learned it so fast I don't know, but in a second we are all singing. We are locked in.

We sing and push and sing and pull some more. I have nothing and I have everything to give. We look at each other without saying a word and understand everything that needs to be understood. My eyes blur as the thought of victory in this immense feat materializes into reality right before my eyes. I've never felt anything like this before. My heart is explosive and my vision is speckled with thousands of tiny stars. I can hardly breathe as we drop the beast over the wall and clamor over to the finish mat. We scream and hug and cry, unfazed by the mixing of sweat and sticky bodies . We had done it!

Dev throws both hands up in the air. "Big Dipper, that's a victory!"

As I catch my breath and drop to the floor, I glance back at the course we have just completed. The impossible seems so much smaller now. Dev and Lilah waste no time debriefing the exercise and inviting us to reflect. We agree that most of us were skeptical at first. But in looking around the group and seeing there were others who needed us, strangers or not, we knew it was bigger than us all.

Big Dipper belts out our new group song on the way to the showers, and I feel an immense surge of pride. "Yee-hoo!" Javier cries, racing towards the bathhouse.

But as proud as I feel, something else lingers here, at this moment. Even in this triumph, as I allow the cool water to flow over my body and decompress from the challenge, my mind wanders off like a lost child. The girl before the challenge wasn't afforded the luxury of getting into her own head. But since the weight of the course has lifted, she drifts, heavy in thought.

I live with the Lizard King. I know him better than anyone could ever know another being. The Lizard King once called me a cow. He hated my body as he hated himself and needed me to know. He loved wielding the magic of his hate, changing words into guns and playing Russian roulette. Eventually, the voice of the Lizard King turns into mine. His thoughts become my thoughts. And those thoughts like to run. And run, and run, and run. Even though at my core I never really believed the Lizard King, never really trusted the beast, he was loud. I cannot speak, I cannot beat him. Our thoughts are marathoners, trained to go the distance. And even now, as a grown child, the Lizard King's voice threatens to steal the courage and faith I have been forced to weave. He is a selfish reptile; he wants it all for himself and for me to have none. Because then I would be indebted to him.

The Lizard King makes the rules of the world, too, and those rules read: *Throw your life away. The only marked path for you is that from which you came.* I cannot imagine a worse fate. It keeps me up at night; it feels etched in stone, so real and so true. I can feel the generations of suffering pressing up against me. The truth is that I start to believe him. He is quite convincing after all.

Though my brain does as brains do—find a smaller, safer place to hide—my soul desires nothing more than to break free. There is nothing else I can do but fight. The wild inside is growing. I need sun and air and rain. It is like breaking out of the matrix. I cannot take the pill, hell, there is no damn pill. Under the weight of the Lizard King, I have to make it myself.

The realization cascades into the shower drain beneath my feet: The Lizard King, in his many forms, will always be there. In the slice of a word, in the face of a stranger, on a platform in the middle of the forest. He says he loves me. He loves me so much he tries to kill me, with shiny fruits from poisoned trees. And even here, on this sacred ground, in this untamed wilderness, the question remains: In the Lizard King's garden, how can I be sure not to eat?

"We don't find ourselves;
we create ourselves."

—George Bernard Shaw

5. FIRE

In the wilderness everything is alive and loud. Even the quietest of things, like the water striders, the tree trunks, and the sunbeams—they all have lungs and speak thunderously, begging you to listen. I have quickly come to love this. The more I notice, the more I notice. When I take a deep breath from a big rush of wind, I imagine it lifting me to the tops of the trees to rest there. It is only the end of the fifth day, but I could stay here forever.

Tonight we will have Community Fire. All of the small camp groups will come together as one to reflect on our time here, and light a traditional bonfire using flint and steel. I've had nothing to lose by coming to this place, that much has been made clear in this short time. I am excited to see if anyone else has changed. I wonder if they, too, have yielded to being lost.

The forest is nearly dark as we walk single file down the hill behind the great hall. Community Fire is held at the most sacred spot on the grounds. It is a rule to walk silently, as the journey is meant to be as pensive as the destination. I love routines. I love things that hold meaning. I love the idea of something so thoughtful.

In my stride, I think back to what Dev told us about time. He was right. Everything that happens here seems suspended in the air or stretched out in the chirps of crickets. Time bends and warps as you wade on the lake or watch dancing fireflies under the moonkissed sky. And I don't resist because I don't want to.

I don't resist because, in this stretching and bending, I become less afraid of what I've been and less afraid of who I want to be. I remember that I have always been the girl who feels, who saves herself, who listens to hear, who wants better for better's sake. That has always been a problem in my family. When you hold up a mirror and people don't like it, they leave you, hurt you, or try to make you small. I haven't heard my voice in many years. But it has been five days, and I think I am beginning to recognize the sound.

We reach our destination, and night has fully fallen. It is pitch black and difficult to see anything at all. We turn on our headlamps, still in silence, and find our seats on wooden logs arranged in a giant circle. In the center of the circle is an enormous stack of logs arranged in a cabin formation and filled with sticks. To the side of the stack lies a small tarp piled with brush and dried pine needles. Ally, a team supervisor, approaches the stack, raises her hand, and waits for stillness. She speaks firmly:

"This is Community Fire. Here, the entire camp community comes together to share space. We light the fire like the people who came before us, those who lived and survived by its hand. We scrape the magnesium onto the pile of pine needles scavenged from the forest. We remain silent as our eldest campers scrape and strike and spark, working hard to ignite a flame to catch the brush. When they are victorious, we celebrate. They then throw the fresh flame in the bonfire, and it comes alive. But when they are not, and they will not be, we hold our presence until they are. We show them we are here in our silent care, in our minds' encouragement, in our hands over our chests or our waving fingers of good energy. Because they courageously model for us what we all come to camp to do—to try and to fail and to push and succeed—to be free. To survive, just like the people who came before us, and like the future people we are working to become. This is a sacred tradition and it must be respected."

A cooler breeze carries her words out over the field, and we shift our bodies in the space. Not a single person speaks, and it is clear that what is understood is understood.

Dev, Lilah, and Ally will lead the ceremony for us tonight. I am so honored to be here, and I am so proud of them. They kneel by the brush pile, meticulously taking turns scraping the magnesium onto the pile of pine needles. The silence is profound; the only sounds that can be heard are the soft scrape of metal and the coo of a faraway mourning dove. I wonder what keeps it awake at this time of night.

As they work, the sense of unity grows among the seated. Yet we aren't doing anything except showing up. We are all here, in this moment, and that is enough. Each strike of the flint sends a tiny bit of hope out into the fire circle. I think everyone can feel it.

Finally, a spark catches. Distant, respectful snaps ripple across the crowd in reaction. A small flame flickers across the brown needles at first; it dances, twirls, and then grows, eventually consuming the pine and everything else on the tarp. A booming cheer erupts from the circle now, breaking the silence with a burst of joy. Instinctively, the firelighters dump the flame into the cabin structure, and the bonfire roars to life. Its amber warmth illuminates the awed faces in the circle.

Ally raises her hand again and the crowd calms down. She speaks again, her voice softer now:

"Thank you for being here with us. This fire symbolizes our journey, not just at camp but in life. Each of us has faced challenges, and has had to conjure up some inner strength to move forward. Like the flame, we started small, unsure, and vulnerable. But with effort, more vulnerability, some support and spirit, we grew stronger and brighter. Let this be a reminder of our resilience, our capacity for growth, for adaptation, for surviving, and thriving. There is a fire in us all. If the fire goes out, so do you."

As if in understanding, the flames of the bonfire rise higher now, sending the shadows from the trees to weave stories in the dirt. I stare into its core. Its heat on my skin reminds me I am alive; it is a tangible marker of where I am, of who I am becoming. I drift like the smoke rising into the night sky and far away into the depths of my mind. There, I see her: the little one, being crushed by invisible pressure, by not being enough for love, burdened by who she isn't and who she may never, ever turn out to be. She is crushed by love that costs her everything that she is. I am her, sitting quietly at the edge of this circle. Her eyes reflect the firelight, wide with wonder and fear. I reach out to hold her, not with my hands, but with my promises. I tell her that we will get through this together. I tell her that she is alright, exactly how she is. I tell her that she is enough. And even through those glassy, glazed-over eyes, she shows a tiny smile.

I hug her tighter than I've ever hugged anyone before. Then she fades into the firelight. I carry her with me. I carry the fire with me, too. I think it has always been there, somehow actually pushing me forward despite everything that's ever happened to me. Its warmth, its light, its power—they are here and they are deep.

The night air cools and the flames surrender to the darkness, leaving behind a smoldering glow. Faces recede in the bushy backdrop, each drifting along their path, each tangled in their reckonings.

I let the stillness wash over me, and the forest holds its breath. I hold my breath too.

There is much more to be done.

"Strength does not come
from physical capacity.
It comes from an indomitable will."

—Mahatma Gandhi

6. WAYFARING

We are halfway through our two-week training before kids arrive, and now comes the ultimate test at Horizon Pines: Wayfare. This rite of passage is a defining experience for all campers. It's the chance to really find the stuff they're made of.

For two to three nights, they will leave Horizon Pines for a quest along a lengthy section of the Appalachian Trail. Campers will both trek and camp the trail, having only what's in their packs and on their backs. Each carries their food, rain gear, and navigation tools—maps and compasses—to guide them. If they run low on supplies, they are expected to adapt. While there is a phone for emergencies, the ultimate goal is to confront oneself, to face the challenge, and to discover who emerges on the other side.

My group is about to embark on a fifteen-mile, three-day journey and I am not feeling one hundred percent confident. I've never undertaken anything like this before. Yet still, in the past five days, I've learned two crucial lessons: difficult tasks are worthwhile, and I am capable of doing them.

Mitch, the Wayfare specialist, greets us as we sidle up to the den where all of the gear for wayfaring is stowed. Rows of old packs, mats, and boots line the cobweb-covered shelves, and we take it all in as he begins the briefing. "Good morning, everyone, and congratulations! You are about to embark on your first Wayfare. You'll be fitted for your trail gear here, including your navigation tools and first aid kit. Then you'll head to the kitchen for other essentials: food, water bottles, and iodine pills. You'll need to rely on maps and compasses to find your way. Fresh water is scarce, so ration carefully. If you run low, you must find the nearest source according to your map and fill all bottles at the stop. The emergency phone is for true emergencies only. This journey is about you versus you. Face the challenge and discover who you are."

As we stuff all of who we'll be for the next three days into our packs, I struggle to adjust to the weight of mine. The thick straps dig into my shoulders, and the pack itself feels like a stone anchor, holding me down. I'm out of breath and out of shape as it is, without the pack. There go those alarm bells again.

We are dropped at the base of Sunrise Mountain. Our set course is to be broken into five-mile stretches—steep, flat, and everything in between—over the next three days. We waste no time and set off, the trail sprawling before us like a ribbon of dust and rock. The sun blazes overhead, casting an unforgiving glare that burns through our hats and into our skin. Sweat trickles down my back, mingling with the dirt already set on my clothes. I take deep breaths, but the heat is unbearable.

Javier, Malik, and Arun are like highschool boys together. They push and shove and see who can get ahead of the other. It's actually endearing. But they are also athletic and fast and quickly move ahead of the group. We pivot and decide to arrange our walking in line form, slowest to quickest.

I am at the front, deliberately so. My pace is a careful negotiation with the terrain. The others fall into a rhythm behind me, their footsteps a steady, comforting cadence. Amelia starts camp songs and we play line games to keep our spirits up. Lilah has us take breaks at the flat places and adds hydration boosters to our bottles. So far, so good (as it can be).

The trail winds through a more dense thicket of trees, their branches forming a canopy that filters the harsh sunlight into dappled patches of yellow on the forest floor.

The occasional bird call echoes in the stillness, a stark contrast to the labored sound of my breathing. I focus on my footsteps, trying to drown out the ugly voices getting louder in the back of my mind:

"You don't think I'll do it? I'll bury you in that backyard. Don't you ever disrespect me again."

"I didn't hit you."

"Stop crying or I'll give you something to cry for."

"You think you more woman than me?"

A sudden sharp incline emerges as we round a rocky corner covered in vines. "I'm sorry guys," I start, "maybe someone else should set the pace for now. This may take a while." The trees loom like silent sentinels, their branches whispering warnings. We rearrange ourselves at my request, but Kya hangs back with me anyway.

"Girl, you know this ain't no thing. Remember high ropes? Take your time. It's not the speed that matters, but the love you give yourself on the way there."

I barely know her, but she sees me. And I see myself. And I climb.

"Keep going!" Arun and Javier cup their mouths and scream to me from above. They cut through the pain like a lifeline.

Pause.

Quiet.

Breathe.

Everyone is well up the hillside by now and the summit is there, I can see it. Just one more step. One more. The ascent is slow, each step a battle against gravity and my exhaustion. The incline demands my full attention, my legs trembling with the effort. My muscles burn, the lactic acid building with every push upward. The Lizard King laughs a booming laugh now. He beats down his gavel like a judge, waiting for my misstep. Today, he will be disappointed.

In one final push that lasts forever, I crest the hill and collapse onto a cool patch of moss. The view stretches out before me—a vast panorama of rolling dips and peaks bathed in the crimson light of late afternoon. It's the golden hour, that perfect time of day when the sun performs just for you. I lie there, gasping for breath while the rest of my group does the same. "That's some good shit, Soda!" Arun playfully slaps me on the back.

Our five miles are done for the day, and we set up camp swiftly before night rushes in. We eat, but we are not full. We are exhausted, but we do not rest. The sounds are new and daunting and wild, yet they call us by name to be here.

Tomorrow there will be another five miles—another battle with the heat, another boxing match with my weight, with my worth—another terrible climb. More and more and more. I hear the Lizard King again as I lie in my sleeping bag. He tells me I can't, but he tells me he loves me, too.

"Fat bull!" I shake my head to get him out.

"You good, So?" Kya notices my shifting and taps my shoulder.

"I'm fine, thanks."

In the vastness of it all, I am alone, and I am not. I am acutely aware of the power I possess to confine myself in my head for life, should I choose to do so.

It's only been a single day of wayfaring.

I don't think that would do me much good.

"You are made by understanding
who you are without your beliefs
about who you should be."

—Andrea Gibson

7. Mirrors

Sleeping in the wild isn't all that bad. I like that the wind can cool my very sweaty skin. And I like that I can see what it does to the leaves on the ground and the flames in our makeshift fire pit. I love that it is invisible yet I can see it, like magic. The wind is lulling me tonight.

It carries the remnants of our fire deep down into my lungs. It sways the big pines back and forth, a slow tick tock, waving me back to the depths of my mind. I am a child again. It is summertime and the air is warm. I am nine. I smell the freshly cut grass and hear the electric hum of cicadas.

"Tag, you're it!" Shai giggles, tapping me on the shoulder before darting away. I chase after my sister, the grass tickling our bare feet as I lunge for her outstretched hand. Around us, the world seems to shimmer and sparkle with endless fun.

The backyard is alive with summer's energy, the air thick with the smell of grilled burgers and sunscreen. A blazing sun beats down on our game in a threatening way, deepening the brown of our melted chocolate skin. As we run barefoot across the lawn, time seems to stretch and bend, each moment unfolding with a languid grace. Then it gives itself over altogether; swaying trees seem to whoop us onward as our screams ring out through the busted fences.

"Can't catch me!" she teases again, laughter trailing behind her like a comet's tail. But I am determined and fueled by the thrill of the chase. When things were good, life was good. When it stormed, it was unbearable. But right now, it was indeed good, and that's all that mattered to me.

"Just you wait!" I close in on her quickly when she suddenly cries, "Look out," pointing at the clouds just behind me.

I whip around, falling for her playful trick, but turn back just in time to see her dart behind a nearby tree. My heart beats in my ears now as I quietly creep up to her hiding place, ready to pounce in a sneak attack, until a distant commotion freezes me in my tracks.

At first, it is just a murmur, a sort of rumbling. But the rumble grows louder and sharper, until it cuts through the air like a knife.

"Hey, what's that?" my sister says as she steps out from her hiding place. I scan the yard as her eyes widen with apprehension. From across the lawn, the voices of our aunts and cousins rise into an angry, blasting screaming match. I feel a knot tighten in my stomach as I listen to the familiar tones twist into something dark and foreign. "It's about time, don't you think? It's only *FAIR!*" my Aunt Beverly exclaims, jabbing her finger in the air and cutting through the shouts with her razor-sharp voice.

Screaming is regular in our house. For no reason. For every reason. You kind of learn to let it move through you.

No speaking.

No protesting.

The big people shout, and the small people listen. But even if there is no shouting, my body is always ready for it. It knows. On any given day, my palms will sweat, my heart will race, my chest will tighten, and I'll feel like crying, and nothing has happened yet. My nine-year-old body has learned this. I am alert. I am ready for war.

But the scene at this backyard barbecue is different, atypical, strange. Strange because Aunt Cee usually tries very hard to keep up appearances around guests. So something is very threatening and very wrong here.

"What's happening?" I whisper to myself, my voice barely audible over the rising tide of noise. No one answers, of course. Instead, Shai and I stand still, our eyes locked on the house where the chaos ensues. Something holds us in place, a sense of impending doom, maybe that roots us to the spot. "Mom?" I call out, my voice trembling as I take a hesitant step forward.

"Mom?" I call out again. Nothing. They can't hear me over their rage.

"You have to tell them the truth," Aunt Frieda hisses back, her words tinged with palpable urgency. "They deserve to know what really happened."

"Well, *I* DIDN'T tell them!" Roland, my older brother, bellows out over the group. "But I know one thing: you can't protect them from the truth forever."

His words hang in the air, heavy with meaning my child's mind cannot grasp. It spins with confusion, trying to make sense of the fragments of conversation drifting to my ears. What truth? What are they talking about? And why does it sound like they're talking about us?

I finally push my way through the charged crowd to see who everyone's talking to.

It's my mother.

Now *I* want answers.

The world around me seems to blur. As the voices rise to a fever pitch, I feel a calming hand on my shoulder. It's my older cousin, Cleo.

"Come on, you two," she says, and leads us cautiously into the house.

By the time we get inside, the screaming has all but stopped. My siblings and I are seated one by one in a row on the floor as my mother takes center stage.

"I HAD Y'ALL FROM IN HERE!!" she screams as she violently points to her stomach. I think I'm in trouble, but I haven't done anything wrong yet. "Sharon did the best she could but couldn't do the job. I stepped up, and I did it! I am your mother! I've been your mother my whole life! She loved you. She just couldn't do it. But believe me, she loved you. No matter what, I AM YOUR MOTHER!"

"Wait..."

The truth plays tag with me now, darting away just when I think I've caught it. I am stumbling to catch up. My stomach knots itself, and gravity lets me go. The world tilts on its axis, and I can feel it. I am floating. I want to throw up. In my mind, everything goes dark. Like I am blindfolded in the middle of the game. And when it lifts, everything I know has changed.

The reality hits me like a tidal wave. The woman I call "Mom" is actually my real mother's sister. My real mother, or should I say my "birth" mother, is my aunt Sharon. Sharon has been part of my life as my aunt all along.

My entire childhood is a lie, a well-intentioned deceit to protect me, but a lie nonetheless. The faces of my siblings, equally stunned and confused, mirror my disorientation. The fragments of my identity scatter over the room in an instant, leaving me to piece together who I really am.

And who I can really trust.

I rock myself to and fro to calm the buzzing in my chest. I am rocking and rocking but feel no change. I have no time to dwell on this. I can't pause my life to figure out who I was, who I am, or where I truly belong. So I just rock—back and forth, swaying like the big pines. They swing wide, sweeping me back to my mat on the open forest floor. The air feels even cooler now, and I am exhausted.

We all can so easily unravel here. I'm certain of that. Surrounded by strangers in these wilds, I feel like that confused child again, trying to find meaning in a world that makes no sense at all.

Kya shuffles in her sleeping bag while Arun's snoring threatens to wake the rest of Big Dipper. Some scurrying little creature snaps a twig on its way home. I am short and quick in my breath. I am damp with sweat. I am vigilant.

"Any minute now," I say softly to myself.

Sooner or later, it will all come crashing down.

"You can feel sad
without chaining yourself to sadness.
You can feel fear
without believing fear is the truth."

—Andrea Gibson

8. Rain

You have no say in becoming one with this wilderness. Moment by moment, you shed the pieces of who you were before you get to the truth. This world consumes you. And there is no pressing pause. Here in this space, your being is broken, and your senses are spread like the toes of a frog. Any shift, any tiny change in the atmosphere, permeates your skin and tells you a message. Then, you start to move differently in response to these signals. It's primal. And there is always something worth taking with you from one breath to the next.

There is rain coming today.

After a breakfast of crumbled granola and instant oatmeal, we gather our packs, roll our mats, and set course for the next five miles. The land doesn't yield any more than it did the day before. But Big Dipper knows better today, and we keep an even, united pace all the same.

Kya pauses, glancing suddenly at the gray clouds forming overhead. "That doesn't look good."

Drip.

Drip.

Drip.

Wet beads pitter-patter lightly. As we continue the steep trek uphill, the sky morphs into thick, gray blankets of wind and grief. The next shelter is still another half mile away. It is time to move quickly.

There is nothing out here to shield me from this rain. A thin poncho is no match for this storm. And I know it is a storm. I can tell by the look of that sky. Storms like to play tricks at first. They are gentle, sweet even at the start; you may enjoy a few drops on your face or a refreshing splash on the back of your neck. The wind may take your breath away or fill you up with the feeling of life. Just as quickly though, they rage, they destroy, and even kill.

I always wonder when God snaps.

In an instant, the sky breaks open. It is relentlessly cold, and wind is suddenly pelting us with frigid, wet beams of water from every angle. My clothes soak through in a matter of minutes and I pray.

"I'm fine,

I'm fine,

I'm fine."

This is just a part of what I came here to do, and I know that. And yet still, in this place, without family or old friends or any comforts at all, the wetness and the cold reach deeper. The temperature drops and the icy water cuts through each layer of clothing like it's parchment paper, then burrows into my skin. It is hard to think of anything else after that. Only the fact that I am miserable.

"Hurry, shelter's not far now, I bet!" Dev shouts over the downpour.

I pray again. To no one in particular. But I do call her the universe.

In the real world, many are afforded the opportunity to escape discomfort, while millions of others are not. This forest is their real life, and out here, it is just that: real. Nature can't be tamed, halted, fixed, or willed away. She does what she feels when she feels it is right. As I succumb to the numbness of the freezing rain, the wind forces my eyes shut. It's dark in here, inside my head. I've met this storm before.

I once knew a hurricane so fierce with no eye. I weathered her, harsh and unpredictable, rageful, cold and draining. I have felt the whip of such a cyclone. And I did survive. Over and over again. And so the only thing I could muster the courage to do in this forest was cry.

"Stop crying before I give you something to cry about!!!" the wind slices into my ears. I jump to cover them and bring my head to my knees. But instead, I hear myself wailing and feel the warm, salty streams slide down my burning cheeks. I cry and hate the rain and wind. I let myself hate them and let myself cry. I welcome the pain with open arms, knowing I have faced her before and have won.

We reach the shelter but I no longer have the desire to escape. My pack falls to the floor, but I remain standing in the greatness of the storm.

The baptism washes my soul clean. My tears take their time. Fear falls away, too, settling in the soil beneath my feet.

I know in my heart that the sky will be clear again.

Because every great storm will eventually pass.

"To live is to suffer;
to survive is to find some meaning
in the suffering."

—Friedrich Nietzsche

9. BRUISED

"I can't believe it's almost over," Malik says, adjusting his blue baseball cap just right. His face is nostalgic, his body tired, but he doesn't want to wish Wayfare goodbye.

I once heard someone say, "Nothing worth doing is easy." Maybe that's why. Maybe he's found something incredible. I think we all have.

Dev and Lilah lead us down the last five miles with steady ease. It's mostly downhill today, thank God. We're all pretty hungry, though. Rationing food and water when you're exerting much more energy than usual is tough, and we've been running low. At least we'll get back to camp today. Then we'll shower and eat a big feast. I can't wait.

We take our final steps down to the parking lot at the last trailhead and complete our fifteen-mile Wayfare. "Group huuuuug!" Javier shouts, pulling us all into his massive, sweaty arms.

"Ewww!" We all laugh and shout and cry a little, too.

When we arrive, the van is already waiting for us, and in no time at all, we are back at Horizon Pines. Once we land, we are quickly ushered to our post-Wayfare nurse check-ins.

"Any concerns at the moment, Soda?" The camp nurse's voice is gentle, but her eyes are sharp and observant as she examines me from head to toe. The medical team is always ready to provide ongoing care for any and everything that could pop up during our time there. They know how taxing the Wayfare can be, both physically and mentally.

"Not really," I say honestly.

"Hmm..." she answers back, confused. "What's this?"

A large, circular, black bruise about the size of a baseball sits in the middle of my left forearm. I didn't notice it until now, and I have never gotten a bruise in my life. That kind of thing just never happens to me. And I have only been out there for a few days. Nothing makes sense about it. Did I bang myself against something? Did something bang against me? Why didn't I feel it? Where did this come from? I don't bruise. I have so many questions for the nurse.

She leans forward, her expression warm and kind. "The truth is, this bruise is a manifestation of the deprivation you've been enduring on the trail. Your body relies on all sorts of things from your food—like vitamins, minerals, proteins—to keep everything ticking along nicely. When it's missing out on those things and working extra hard, it can't do its job properly. And sometimes, that shows up as little warning signs, like this bruise."

Something in me twists up in her language. "Deprivation..." It hasn't actually dawned on me the severity of what I'm experiencing here. For a while now, it's just seemed like a new normal—part of what I signed up for. But seeing these physical abnormalities that have never, and I mean NEVER, happened to me in my lifetime suddenly appear causes a profound internal shift.

The nurse continues, her voice empathetic and calm. "When the body is subjected to prolonged periods of strain, it begins to show signs of distress. Bruising, like the one you have here, is just one way in which the body communicates its struggle to cope with the challenges it faces. Out here, you cannot heal faster than you hurt because you just don't have what you need in the tank to get you there. And the longer you remain in this state, the worse it will get. That is, until you move on to a healthier place where you can get your needs met."

Her words seep into my bruise like water on a sponge. I feel like a turtle with no shell. Vulnerable. But strong, too. Yes, strong. But exhausted.

"As resilient as the human body may be," she concludes, "it's not immune to the toll that such conditions can take. But recognizing these signs is the first step in understanding the depth of the reality you're living."

The reality I'm living...

"Get out, get out. GET. OUT!!" Aunt Cee's screams pierce through the halls of my childhood home as she hurls my little sister's belongings down the stairs. I am there again in an instant. Without thinking. Without trying.

"Ornery, disgusting, nasty, disrespectful bitch. You want to be grown? GET THE FUCK UP OUT OF MY HOUSE!"

I'll never forget that day. It remains to be seen whether or not it will forget me. I am visiting home to get my wisdom teeth pulled and heal for a few days before heading back to college. My little sister Shai, only fifteen, has yet again found herself on the receiving end of one of Aunt Cee's infamous raging rampages.

I am convinced Shai reminds Cee of herself. How could you so deeply hate someone you chose to love if they don't reflect what you could not learn to accept? Sure, she is a troubled kid—doesn't always get good grades and occa-sionally runs with the wrong crowd—but that's normal kid stuff. She is just trying to be a kid. Mistakes are sup-posed to happen.

Like the rest of my siblings, she struggles to cope with our reality of things. Especially because, somehow, she always ends up being the wrong child. Have you ever seen the movie Encanto? She is Bruno. Scapegoated at every turn, blamed for everything wrong that could ever happen to anyone, including herself. Any crowd she'd end up running with, any terrible grade, any street fight or dirty toilet or uncleaned dish or unmade bed or opened window when the heat is blasting warrants a two-hour screaming lecture about how ungrateful and evil she is. This is all of our lives actually, every day. But it's hers even worse in particular. It is almost an obsession, but one seemingly fueled by hate. The good in her is nearly impossible for Cee to see. And my sister knows that. She knows it very well.

On this particular day, the storm is bad. I can feel the queasiness and anxiety swirling up from my chest to my throat. I am so tired of this. I am too old for it. And to this day I'm still not even sure what my sister did to warrant such an unbelievable display of pure rage. Not that it matters.

Aunt Cee screams at the top of her lungs, over and over again, desperately seeking control and order. "GET THE HELL OUTTA HERE. YOU THINK YOU KNOW BETTER THAN ME? YOU MORE WOMAN THAN ME? YOU THINK YOU TOUGH?

GET YOUR STINKING, SELFISH, UNGRATEFUL ASS OUT OF MY DAMN HOUSE. I WILL BURY YOU IN THE BACKYARD. I'LL SHOW YOU WHO'S GROWN."

Over the second-floor railing, clothes, shoes, and books rain down. I am laying down in my bed, one day post-op, sleeping before it all begins. My little sister is trying to stop Aunt Cee from tossing her valuables, but it is really no use. Aunt Cee is in a blind rage, and there is no calming the beast once it's been awakened.

Up until this point, for my entire life, I have been trained to shut up and listen. "Don't say hate. You don't hate anything. Hate is a strong word." I have been brainwashed into pure compliance despite feeling my own fury growing inside at the regular injustices we are forced to endure. I am taught how to stand back and how to stay silent. How to take it. How to relinquish my voice and power. I am trained to accept this as normal, as law. And there is nothing I can say or do to change that.

But I am eighteen now. I have been in the world, and I have seen it. I have learned self-government. I am no longer a child. I practice speaking and listening and learning the sweet, gentle tone that my vocal cords produce. I know myself, even if only a little. And I hear myself cry out through mangled jaw and bloody cotton balls,

"STOP!"

Aunt Cee is just about to launch my little sister's computer over the banister when I grab it from the top. She doesn't like that and attempts to wrestle it from my hands, but I won't let go. The next moment comes in a blackout.

Still clutching the laptop with one hand, she winds back her fist and punches me clean in the center of my swollen, stitched face. I cry. I don't know what to do but cry.

"You punched me!" I struggle to speak through tear-filled cotton balls.

"No, I didn't!"

The next few moments are a blur. Just like my bruise lights a warning sign for me, this punch to the face tells me to leave and never come back. I have been beaten countless times before, but this is different. I am eighteen. I am an adult. I've just had oral surgery. She doesn't care. This isn't about my sister or about me. The reality is starkly clear: I have to run.

"Can you please come get me? My mother punched me in the face," I cry through puffy eyes and a still bleeding mouth. On the other side of the phone is my favorite person, Anne, the wife of my old high school English teacher Nate, and to me, family.

A few years ago, my connection with Anne became specific, sudden, and beautiful—like a child meeting their mother. We love each other, and I open my heart to her over the years that I am in school. She knows Aunt Cee is unstable, but she has never seen me through something like this before. I trust her and her entire family with everything I ever am, right down to my core. It is scary at first, being loved by her. I don't find love that's free, without conditions—not in my house. Still, she is that for me, and the first person I think to call. She arrives in less than ten minutes with Nate as the driver. They wait for me to grab whatever I can. I race around the house, furiously trying to bag my life up in an instant. I feel nothing and everything. I am numb and confused and desperate. Having what I think is enough, they scoop me up and take me to their home. I will never return to stay again.

The choice to leave makes itself. And after that, the world becomes gray and confusing, and unbearable for many years. I will have to learn to risk and risk again for love by wading through the murky waters of my history. These waters want so desperately to drown me. The guilt of surviving will poke holes in my life raft; I'll spend countless years inflating and reinflating it with my own breath. I'll run out of breath. I'll sink and swim and then sink again. I'll lose consciousness; I'll turn my consciousness off, and I'll become lost, deep beneath the surface of the water. And I'll breathe again. And I'll float again.

Whatever it takes to be free.

"For small creatures such as we,
the vastness is bearable only through love."

—Carl Sagan

10. STARS

To the One Who Will Choose Me,

Sometimes I think about how we'll be under the same stars, you and I, even when we're worlds apart. It's funny how something so vast and so far away can make me feel close to you. When I look up at the little specks, I imagine they're somehow guiding me to you, to the love that will keep me going in this life. I search each tiny piece of light in the indigo sky for your voice, your face, and your hands. And I find them.

One day I bet we'll vow to keep our evening tradition of stargazing, no matter where we are. I'm practicing now actually, right this minute. I imagine our first stargazing together will be at this very camp, maybe, on the front steps of the great hall or down by the lake. It will be chilly and smell like trees. Fireflies will make us more stars. And maybe you'll tell me you love me.

The air here at camp is fresh and cool. It reminds me that I am alive. It lifts my chin to the sky to see the stars, and then I think of you. All the time, I think of you. You will be the greatest home I've ever known. I am quite sure about that. Because I am so open to love.

Right now, the camp hums quietly around me, yet it feels like a void. There are people here, yet at times I still feel alone. Even when they are present, it is as though they are not. I find myself slipping into places, deep hidden cracks in my mind that I've not had the time to go to. This place performs such sad magic in that way. It takes me back to every island I've ever lived on, every lone wilderness I've ever held inside.

I never told you this, my love, but I will tell you now. I was shipwrecked once there—inside my mind, torn apart by a chaotic hurricane of a person. I was sailing across the ocean when the storm destroyed my boat, an unlucky sailor in a bad storm.

At first, I panicked. Debris flew everywhere, my clothes were torn, and I had no real sense of where I was anymore. It was all just gray and windy. But I managed to find a life raft. My brothers and sisters were there too, and I tried to help them. I called out for them, showed them the life raft. I swam to them with all my might, desperate to save them from the chaos around us. I screamed at them to grab hold of the raft so we could swim to shore. But they wouldn't, they didn't even want to swim. I screamed, cried, and raged because I knew the island was right there. I could see it, and I knew it was wild but safe. My legs and lungs burned from the effort, but I couldn't bear to see them drown, so I pulled their arms around my waist and swam for them. But they were too heavy, maybe too hurt, and they didn't want to swim.

The hurricane was fierce and raging, and I was running out of time. With a heavy heart and tears streaming down my face, I let them go. The island was right there, and it was good, and I had to get there. Though my heart surely left my chest and my whole body trembled, I swam until I reached the rocky shore. Alone.

Sharp sand grains filled my fingernails as I crawled up onto the banks of the dark, foresty place. I turned over to see if my family was coming. They were not. They were screaming and crying and scared, but they did not follow me. They were not coming. I stayed on the island for many days, and I survived. I found food and made shelter and stayed dry.

For the first few days, I spent hours at the shore, screaming out into the ocean. The storm was over, but I could still see them. Day by day, big waves pushed them further out to sea. They struggled to tread water. The storm would come back every now and then, bigger and louder, and they would float away faster than before. Eventually, I grew too tired and sad to scream for them. They did not want to swim, and I could not make them. So, I chose to leave the shore and move inland.

Shortly after, I heard voices—kind and curious voices. It turns out I wasn't the only one living in this new place. They were locals, and they showed me how to thatch a better roof for my shelter and catch food that was more filling. They taught me how to build a stronger foundation for my home and to catch rainwater to store for later.

After many months of getting to know them, I told them how I wasn't supposed to be there alone, that I had lost my family. I cried because it still hurt so badly, because I was angry and sad, or both. They understood because they had been shipwrecked too. It was nice to be shipwrecked together. We had all chosen that place, and it was nice to be there with one another. I realized that maybe I was supposed to arrive there alone.

I'm glad I decided to swim that day many years ago. I learned about food and shelter, but also about choices and choosing. Sometimes you have no choice and every choice at the same time. Sometimes you must choose yourself to make it.

But I also found out you can choose other people, and they can choose you back. It doesn't matter where you are from or how many scars you have. You can choose to be together, even for the rest of your life.

I wanted to let you know how much I really am thinking of you right now. I bet you were shipwrecked too, once, in many ways. But already, in advance, I love you deeply.

That's why I search each tiny piece of light in the indigo sky for your voice, your face, and your hands. And I am so glad that I find them. I am so very glad that we will choose each other.

Love always,
Sodasia

"It's hard to tell who has your back,
from who has it long enough
just to stab you in it."

—Nicole Richie

11. Betrayed

"How are you?" My Aunt Cee asks as she lowers her large frame onto our childhood couch in her living room. I am twenty-one years old and haven't slept in this house or sat on this couch for many years. But today, for some reason, I woke up and decided that today would be the day I tell my Aunt Cee how much she has hurt me.

"Well..." I don't know where I find the nerve. I guess I've always had it buried deep inside. But it was suppressed my entire life, and I'm tired of that. I refuse to deny my reality any longer. My body has known all these years what my brain can now articulate.

"I've been really hurt for quite some time. It's hard to put into words. I think you were doing your best, as you always used to say, in raising us. But I think you were stressed and having a hard time. Growing up here was difficult. The things you said, the names you called me, the screaming, the guilt-tripping because you had rescued us...

And the last time we were together, I was really hurt by what you did. How you hit me, and all the other times you did too... and not just that, but..."

She stares at me, but I can't stop my word vomit. It feels so good yet so risky. I think, any moment now, the storm will strike. Here it comes. I flinch. Here it comes. I sweat. But I keep talking, not stopping until there's nothing left to say. Then, I wait for the storm to come.

It doesn't.

She shifts her weight in awkward silence as I catch my breath. I'm acutely aware of every movement—every crease in her face, every bend in her hands, every shift of her body. I am bracing myself.

"I never realized..." she starts, "...I'm sorry."

I am in shock. Did she actually hear me? Did she actually listen to what I was saying? She seems to understand. After all these years, it seems... she actually does. I am apprehensive, but not crying, hiding, screaming, or hating myself. This new feeling is welcome. Scary, but welcome.

I sit with her words for a while, really hoping she means them. The little girl inside me cries a ferocious cry, but I remain composed.

After what feels like an eternity, she breaks the silence. "I hear you. And you're right. It's been so hard trying to take care of everyone. Like your brother. He's in jail again and needs some new clothes. I don't know how I'm going to get him those new clothes..."

She turns toward me intently. "Can I borrow $200?"

Pause.

Quiet.

Breathe.

Today is Lake Swim. At the end of each session, campers who have passed their deep swim test are offered the challenge to swim the lake. Not the whole lake, really, just across from the boys' side dock to the girls' side dock. It's a great expanse, difficult but not impossible.

Camp is all about the limits or learning you set for yourself. I've quickly discovered that I am the decider in life. I always have a choice. I can choose to feel like things are possible. I can choose to hand my anxiety a paintbrush and let him coat the back of my eyes in red tempura. I can choose hope.

I take my mark from the boys' side dock. A few other counselors in training have decided to join me, including Arun and Kya. There's also Randall, the lifeguard, guiding us on his red floaty and cheering folks on the other side. I have no floaty, but I trust myself.

I take a big leap into the chilly water and welcome the sensation. Everyone follows suit, and we place our hands on the dock, waiting for the signal.

Pause.

Quiet.

Breathe..

Randall blows his whistle, and we are off.

For the first ten yards, I'm fine; I'm crushing it. But then everything starts to hurt. There's stinging in my toes that runs up my calves, into my back, and lands at the base of my neck. I stretch my arms to the side as the gentle rocking of the waves spreads it to my fingertips.

But that's okay because I've invited pain to be my teacher, my pusher. I close my eyes and drift away to the deepest pains I've ever felt in life. Oh yes, I've felt pain worse than this. So I can push a little more. I can go a little longer.

My father. Who is he? Where could he have been all these years? What was more important to him than me? Does he know my name? What are the features of his face? I look nothing like my mother. I don't even have her skin. I must look like him, yet I've never laid eyes upon him. Does he even have a name? Is he dead?

I can go a little longer.

My siblings. My family. Drifting away, so far, so much further than I can bear. Lost for good, it feels. I am alone. Truly alone.

I can go a little longer.

And then there is my mother.

'Mother' is the word that rips me up. Mother. Aunt? I have been split. I am two people. I am a daughter and a niece, half and half. And because of that, it feels like I am no one's anything.

My mother. My Aunt Cee. She loves me. She loves me so much that she tells me so. She loves me so much that she has stuffed me in the tiniest box and wishes to keep me there.

But in doing so, she denies me.

A wave pushes me once more, shooting the deep sting through my core up into my throat. I want to scream, but I don't.

"Don't scream, or I will give you something to scream for!"

I do not scream. If I scream, she will deny me.

I turn onto my back and float, praying for some air in the next deep breath.

Aunt Cee raises her eyebrows in a soft way, and I feel confused by many things now. "Can I trust you?" I ask myself. I haven't been able to all these years, despite how desperate I've been to try. But she seems to hear me now. She seems to see me too, at least more than she did before. But this feels like such a big ask, especially when I haven't been here for years, and we are having a twenty-one-years-late conversation. I ask myself again: Can I trust you?

I remember the boundary-setting my therapist and I have been working on and say, "I'll think about it." Then I get up to leave. She hugs me, and I hug her back. I thank her for listening. Later, in the car on the way home, I call her and tell her the money will be sent the next day. She thanks me. Then she says she wants to spend more time together. My world is shifting again in a strange way. I'm not sure what any of this means...

I can see the other dock about fifteen yards away, but there is nothing left in me by now. My heart may burst. I am tired, trembling, and empty. Just one last push. I can go a little longer.

Aunt Cee sends me inspirational memes every morning. It's been a week since I lent her the money, and she's been extra nice to me. I don't respond. I'm still processing our conversation. I'm not sure what to feel, really. Maybe she has changed...

The girls' side dock casts a shadow over my face as I grab its edge. I made it, by the skin of my teeth I made it. I pull myself up onto the wooden platform as the cheers from my friends ring out across the water. I smile so widely, in disbelief at what I just accomplished. And suddenly, with no warning, my body and head smack down onto the dock. The world goes dark.

Ping! You have one new text message:

Aunt Cee: I SENT YOUR MONEY BACK BY WESTERN UNION. YOU CAN PICK IT UP TODAY. AND I'VE BEEN THINKING ABOUT WHAT YOU SAID TO ME LAST WEEK. ABOUT WHAT I DID. AND IT'S NOT TRUE AT ALL. I DID THE BEST I COULD WITH ALL OF Y'ALL. I NEVER HURT YOU. I NEVER LAID A HAND ON YOU. I TOOK Y'ALL WHEN I DIDN'T HAVE TO AND DID THE BEST I COULD. I DON'T UNDERSTAND WHERE YOU GET ALL THOSE LIES FROM. JUST MAKING UP LIES. WHERE DO YOU EVEN GET THAT FROM? WHY WOULD YOU PUT ME THROUGH SOMETHING LIKE THAT? IT'S SO HURTFUL. MAKING ME THINK I'M A BAD MOM. I REALLY DON'T GET IT. YOU'RE THE ONE WITH THE PROBLEM. I DON'T HAVE A PROBLEM. YOU'RE A LIAR. YOU HAVE ALWAYS BEEN A LIAR. I DON'T WANNA HAVE THIS DISCUSSION ANYMORE, SODASIA...

People don't talk enough about family heartbreak. To do so would normalize it and make it more real. It is not like being dumped by a boy. It is not like getting rejected after a first date. It is not like losing a friend. It's closer to the grief of death. Not just of them but of you too... like losing a piece of your life. When the people who have attended the thousands of births of who you are becoming betray you when they drive the knife through your willingly open heart, you cannot breathe. You cannot even cry. There is nothing you can do but lose that part of your life, the part that lived in the trust they snatched from your soul.

I look at the words in the text message and do not move. It is 5:01 pm on a warm Friday afternoon, and I am sitting in my Jersey City apartment. My husband calls me from the kitchen for dinner, but I do not respond. He calls again, but I cannot say a word. Finally, he enters the back room in a huff, asking me what's wrong. I hand him my phone. He reads the message. Then, saying nothing, he swallows me in a deep, compressing hug. The dam inside of me bursts. I know these are the last words I will ever exchange with the woman I once called "mother." There is no other choice. I will mother myself on my own, for good.

I do not judge the tears. I let them fall like cleansing rain. I have spent long enough exchanging my value for silence.

My friends surround me as I come to, a few minutes later. I stand without falling and lean on their shoulders as they escort me off the dock. I rest, eat, and thank them. They hug and thank me back.

"Why the hell are you thanking me?" I half-laugh into my orange juice. Kya squeezes my shoulder and hugs me one more time.

"For showing us how to try."

There is so much good in the world too.

And I'll always intend to find it.

"Humans are nightshades.
They grow in the dark."

—Andrea Gibson

12. THE PRICE OF FREEDOM

I am twenty-six. Five years have passed. I have been married to the love of my life for all five of those years. I am a grown woman now.

For so many of those years, though, I've felt a significant absence, a noticeable emptiness within me. I've stood on the shores of my mind's island, watching the world go by—not just observing, but living too, and quite well, at that. But living alone, without my family.

Yet amidst the loneliness, painful as it has been, I've unearthed something magical. Someone I hadn't realized was missing until I began wading through the deafening silence left by my family's absence...

Me.

I discovered myself. I began to understand who I was and recognize the unique timbre of my own voice in moments of joy or excitement. I started to grasp where I've been and where I want to go. Memories of my family accompany me: the happy ones that soften me, and the somber ones that pushed me onward.

I've also deepened friendships with people who became family, enriching my life in ways I hadn't known before. They chose to understand me deeply and fill my days with genuine, unconditional love. And the best, most beautiful part? It was me they chose. The real me. I didn't retreat because of my imperfections, and neither did they. I leaned in with every fiber of my being because there was everything to gain and nothing to lose, and all the love I could ever need right there for me. And they continue to teach me that, time and again, love is worth the risk.

The long yellow school buses funnel down the grassy hill one by one, each filled with smiley, bouncing children. It is a sticky, hot day in June of 2016, the best type of day for them to start the summer of their lives. I wonder where they've come from, and I worry about where they're going. But I don't worry about this moment right now. Because right now, we are all free. We are free to be our worst and our best and define our own names. We are free to forget or to go back, to live, to fear, and to believe. We are free to be here, just to be.

The excitement is palpable as the kids practically rip their luggage from the back of the bus and race to the counselors who hold their names on white signs. Through the back of the last bus window, I see two puffy black braids neatly tied with red bo-bos. The little girl wearing them has glassy eyes and folds her arms tightly around her shoulders. I smile at the driver through the open doors. She looks into her rearview, then back at me, and nods me onward.

The girl sees me coming but does not unfold her arms. I notice a sweet little black doll wrapped tightly underneath them. I smile and set myself down next to her in silence. We don't speak. We just breathe.

Eventually, she turns to look at me.

"She can come to camp too, you know," I say, pointing at her beautiful black doll. It looks just like her now that I see it up close.

"Really?" she asks, raising her eyebrows innocently. I nod back, and she stands up slowly, seemingly ready to go.

I stick out my hand and offer a shake.

"My name is Soda. Welcome to Horizon Pines."

"Strong Back, Soft Front, Wild Heart."

—Brene Brown

13. FOUND

"I think I'm ready now. No matter what happens, I'll be okay." It's summertime on Long Island, the place I grew up, and my chosen family gathers around me as I stare at the unopened email.

The subject line reads, *"Your results are in..."*

My present to myself on my twenty-seventh birthday last month was one of those ancestry DNA kits. The kit will tell me where on Earth I'm from, where my family's from, what percent of which ethnicity I am, and match me with potential family members. Flowers are blooming everywhere this May. They pop brightly with their yellows and reds and purple hues. And I am not afraid of finding nothing.

I am finally ready to connect more pieces of my puzzle. I have spent so much time in the dark of my own identity because of the choices of others. But now that I know who I am, who I choose to be, I am ready to learn more. I am ready to choose more, to paint a picture of myself that is full of colors and clarity. It is time to solve mysteries. And nothing can break me more than I've already been broken.

I click the email open and the information starts to flood across the page. I am Nigerian! Wow! And a lot of it. Cameroon, Congo, West Bantu Peoples... I am beautifully African. Though in truth, I've always known that.

"Let's see, Parent one information... Nigerian, Congo, Mali..." Much the same as me of course. But I trail off as I see the graph below this one.

"Parent two..."

There's information here from my other half. My deepest unfulfilled wish of knowing anything about my father is changing right now. The room seems to go fuzzy as I click through dropdown menus and scan graphs, scouring the information for clues about his identity. Nigeria, Ivory Coast, Ghana, Congo, Mali...

But no name. No picture. Still, it is unbelievable to have so many new pieces of my tapestry right here in front of me.

Ping! You have a new message in your inbox.

*"Potential matches for **first cousins** or half-siblings: You share forty percent DNA with...*

Dorian Marshall

Lilian Jameson

Aaryn Jacobs
Ray Coolidge.
Send them a message to connect today!"

"Half siblings..." But I know my biological mother's side of things. I grew up with enough aunties and uncles to know all six of her children. My mother's family knew most things about her—except who she had conceived me with.

I try not to get my hopes up, but the earth is still tilting, and the room is even fuzzier now. I calm my nerves long enough to draft a message to Dorian. I expect nothing, but I hope that he will respond.

Hi Dorian! I hope you are well. I noticed you and I share quite a bit of DNA, and I was hoping to chat with you. I understand this can be awkward. Does the name Lilian Jameson mean anything to you? She is in your family tree as well as mine. I'm not looking for anything in particular, just to learn more about myself and help others in the process if I can. I appreciate any response.

After more research I realize we are all in each others' digital family trees. The world is getting smaller by the minute. I copy and paste the same message to Lilian Aaryn and Ray with a few tweaks. No harm no foul. I have nothing to lose.

But it is **Aaryn's** message that sends my heart soaring:

Well hi there, Sodasia! It seems that we're indeed siblings. I actually found Lilian on here a few years back, and it seems she's already reached out to **Dad**. We will help you fill in your story. Nothing awkward about how we roll, I can promise you that.

Dad.

Is it really? It can't be. Is it all happening this quickly? No. Too good to be true. I push the excitement to the back of my mind. I do not want to be disappointed.

Word travels fast amongst these new strangers... siblings? They all believe I am their sister. Two seconds of knowing me, and they tell me they know my father. They had been through this whole shebang before with Lilian, so they have no doubts. This is all beginning to sound crazy to me. But I can't stop the carnival ride from twisting. I'm on it now, strapped in, sticking to the walls by the gravity of the loops and turns. There is no turning back now. I remind myself that I am not afraid of finding nothing.

Ping! You have a new message in your inbox:

Ray sent you an image. Click here to download.

Click.

This is Frank Collins. He is your father. If you're up for it, he'd like to talk with you on video chat tomorrow afternoon. He says he wants to meet his daughter.

"Wow."

The man's smile is mine. His eyes are mine, too. His cheeks are undeniably those that rest on my face. Even if I want to deny it, I cannot. I try to. For my own sake. To slow the paradigm shift happening inside of my brain just a little.

I turn the computer around so my family can see the image. Their eyes grow wide. They look at me. Then they look at him.

And they know it, too.

After all these years.

He is found.

"To find yourself, think for yourself."

—Socrates

EPILOGUE

The paternity test office has four clean white walls, one matte ceiling, and one shiny floor. In the middle sits a brown desk, and behind it a kind woman types our information into a database. It has been three days since I video chatted with my father. He says he believes I am his. He is willing to take a paternity test.

A stranger, a paternity test, with a random woman he met online. How could he be so sure?

"You'll get your results in one week," the woman says sweetly. "Good luck."

We leave the facility and climb into his oversized, jet-black Jeep Grand Cherokee. He wants to take me out for pizza. I tell him that sounds nice.

"I knew of your mother, Sharon. Yes. We ran in the same circles," he says, pulling out of the parking lot and onto the main road.

This made sense to me because I knew of my biological mother's past. I ask him to tell me everything. He spares no details in recounting his experience in the war, his struggle with addiction, and the many obstacles he has spent his life working to overcome.

He also tells me that he has been sober for over twenty years. Then he tells me people don't come back from the substance he's used. I am thinking of my mother, whose death was due to complications of her own addiction. I am sad for her. But I am happy for him. In fact, I am proud. His resilience is remarkable.

We pull up to the pizza shop, eat our slices, and then head down to Robert Moses Beach, field five. We sit in the car, silently, watching the waves and the seagulls. The joyful screams and splashes of children ring out over the glistening yellow sand.

"You know," he starts again, "I am going to tell you something that might break your heart. But I don't mean to. I hope you know that."

"It's okay," I answer back, "I want to know everything you have to tell me. I have spent long enough not knowing anything."

"The thing is, even though I knew your mother. I mean, I knew of her... I cannot remember a single time we interacted or a single time we talked. Not once."

I sat thoughtfully, considering his words.

"...I didn't know you existed. If I had I would have tried my best to be there for you. Especially since hearing about your life and everything you have gone through. You didn't need me, clearly. What I mean to say is... you turned out great. And that's no part because of me. But I would have been there if I had known. But I had no idea..."

I feel conflicted inside. I feel proud and strong, but also angry and upset. But I don't want to feel angry or upset. Those emotions feel pointless right now. So I just listen.

"But I don't want you walking the earth thinking that just because I don't remember your mother, somehow you weren't supposed to be here. I don't want you to think you have no meaning in this world.

In fact, thinking back to your birthday, tracing nine months back to just about the time of your conception, I can tell you this. That was the time I hit rock bottom. I totally bottomed out. But something inside me switched. Something changed. I don't know what but a switch went off inside of me. And I decided right then and there I would quit for good. Cold turkey. I would get my life back, my health back. And now that I see you, now that you are standing in front of me, I realize that magic may have been you."

I watch the waves roll and crash and roll and crash. I sink into his words and search my thoughts for somewhere safe to land. But the thought of being unplanned bubbles up in front of me. The thought of being unthought of. Or an afterthought. Or no thought at all.

And then it happens—a movie cuts into my mind. The memories flood my senses like a gritty, sepia-toned indie film.

All of my triumphs,

all of my mistakes,

all of my losses,

all of my grief.

They made me. And what he says does not take away from that. My life has had meaning because I have lived and loved and lost. It isn't defined by circumstance, and the quiet strength that led him to turn his life around lives inside me, too.

I turn to him, and for the first time, I see not just a man who shares my DNA, but someone who has fought battles I may never fully comprehend. His admission, though stark and unsettling at first, now feels like a gift.

We drive back over the bridge towards home with the windows down. My eyes are stinging, but not in a painful way. He drops me at my house, and we share a brief hug.

"Thank you," I say as we pull apart.

Four days later, a tightly sealed, white envelope arrives in my mailbox. It is from the paternity test center. My family gathers around the table as I rip the letter open with the key of my car.

Frank Collins, probability of paternity:

99.9 percent.

ACKNOWLEDGEMENTS

I'd like to thank Quill Hawk Publishing for their thoughtful partnership and professional services. I'd like to thank my friends for holding space for all that I am and rallying behind the many things I set out to accomplish. To my family: Terri, Matt, Rainer, and Atticus, thank you for supporting and loving me unconditionally, at all times and without question. A huge thank you to Matt Pasca for taking the time to provide me with key guidance and feedback at several stages of this writing process. And to my wonderful husband, Danrley, thank you for everything that you are and for holding me up when I simply could not do it myself. I love you.

ABOUT THE AUTHOR

Sodasia Thompson is a passionate writer whose story-telling delves deep into the human experience, exploring themes of loneliness, pain, grief, empowerment, and self-discovery. She is married and works as a special education teacher, infusing empathy and insight into her daily work. Sodasia also has a deep love for music and the arts, which extends to songwriting, music performance, and enjoying Broadway shows.

Her unique narrative style intertwines real-time experiences with reflective flashbacks, crafting stories that profoundly resonate with readers. In 2023, she showcased her resilience and determination as a contestant on Season 46 of the CBS hit reality TV show, *Survivor*, which later aired in 2024. Sodasia Thompson's work is a testament to the healing power of storytelling and its ability to connect and inspire.

For her.